Who Was Lewis Carroll?

by Pam Pollack and Meg Belviso

illustrated by Joseph J. M. Qiu

Penguin Workshop
An Imprint of Penguin Random House

To Mark Aaron Polger, Keith Saks,
and Oliver Polger—PP

For Eeyore's—more than a bookstore—MB

PENGUIN WORKSHOP
Penguin Young Readers Group
An Imprint of Penguin Random House LLC

The publisher does not have any control over and does not assume any responsibility for author or third-party websites or their content.

Text copyright © 2017 by Pam Pollack and Meg Belviso. Illustrations copyright © 2017 by Penguin Random House LLC. All rights reserved. Published by Penguin Workshop, an imprint of Penguin Random House LLC, 345 Hudson Street, New York, New York 10014. PENGUIN and PENGUIN WORKSHOP are trademarks of Penguin Books Ltd. WHO HQ & Design is a registered trademark of Penguin Random House LLC. Printed in the USA.

Library of Congress Cataloging-in-Publication Data is available.

ISBN 9780448488677 (paperback)   10 9 8 7 6 5 4 3 2 1
ISBN 9780515159318 (library binding)   10 9 8 7 6 5 4 3 2 1

Contents

Who Was Lewis Carroll?

On July 4, 1862, a small boat sailed down the Isis River—a part of the famous Thames—in Oxford, England. Three sisters, Lorina, Alice, and Edith Liddell, were enjoying a day on the water with family friends Robinson Duckworth and Charles Dodgson. The two men taught at Oxford University with Mr. Liddell, the girls' father.

Charles Dodgson was like no other adult the girls knew. He was very smart. He taught math at the university. He loved to invent puzzles and games. He took dozens of photos of the girls dressed up in costumes with a very new invention: the camera.

But best of all, Charles told great stories. He often made them up on the spot, taking ideas from real life and making them seem funny or magical. As he rowed the boat that day, Charles made up a story about a girl—also named Alice—who chased a white rabbit into its hole and fell into a strange, wonderful new world.

In this world, many of the characters seemed a lot like the people in Alice Liddell's own life, only funnier. Everyone in the boat inspired a character in the story. A duck for Reverend Duckworth, an imaginary bird called a Lory for Lorina, and an Eaglet for Edith. Charles himself was represented by a Dodo. This was not too surprising because he had a slight stutter. Sometimes when he said his last name it came out Do-do-dodgson.

Charles's friend Duckworth was amazed that Charles could make up such an enchanting story so quickly. Later that day, Alice wondered: Could Charles write the new story down so she could read it again and again? Charles sometimes wrote and published poetry and essays under a made-up name (called a pen name), Lewis Carroll.

But he had never been asked to write a children's story. He promised Alice he would.

The world is lucky that Alice Liddell asked for that favor! Because the story Charles wrote as Lewis Carroll became one of the most famous children's stories of all time: *Alice's Adventures in Wonderland.*

CHAPTER 1
Fun and Games

Charles Lutwidge Dodgson was born on
January 27, 1832. His father was a country
parson. Just like a priest, he was in charge of the
local church.

Charles's home life in Daresbury, England, was very religious. The family read the Bible and went to church often. When Charles was born, he already had two older sisters. Over time his parents would have eleven children in all, seven girls and four boys. Almost all of them had a stutter like Charles, who was also deaf in his right ear.

Charles loved his life in Daresbury. His mother was very patient and kind. His brothers and sisters were a lot of fun. Charles was a curious boy who wanted to learn about the world. He climbed trees and played with frogs.

His father taught him math, reading, and even how to speak Latin. One day when Charles was very young, he brought his father a book of advanced math equations and asked, "Please, explain." His father told him he was too young to understand such complicated things. Charles nodded and said, "*But*, please explain!"

Croft Rectory

When Charles was eleven, his father moved the family to Saint Peter's Church in Croft, in the north of England. They moved into the Croft Rectory, a house especially for the parson and his family, in 1843. It was much bigger than the house in Daresbury, and stood across the street from the large stone church of Saint Peter's. Charles's father built a real schoolhouse to replace the barn that had been used for lessons. Parson Dodgson taught the students himself.

Life in the Dodgson home was centered on the family's strong faith. Family prayers were said in the morning and evening. On Sundays everyone read the Bible. Charles tried very hard to live up to what he thought God might want of him.

But life was also a lot of fun. The Dodgson children all loved to play games, and Charles was especially good at coming up with exciting things to do. He put on puppet shows in a theater he built himself. He performed magic tricks.

He acted out plays and stories. He drew funny pictures.

Charles was so fascinated by the big train that ran near Croft, he even built his own version out of a wheelbarrow and a barrel. Then he set up areas in the garden that stood for different stations. He drove his brothers and sisters from station to station, stopping for snacks at each one.

To get on the train, they had to buy a ticket. Charles made up a strict timetable for the train and anyone who broke the rules—say, by jumping out of the train while it was moving—was put in jail.

Charles and his siblings loved their new home so much that they wanted to leave parts of themselves in the home forever. So one day they lifted up some of the floorboards to hide some small treasures underneath—a handkerchief, a thimble, a glove. Charles added a block of wood.

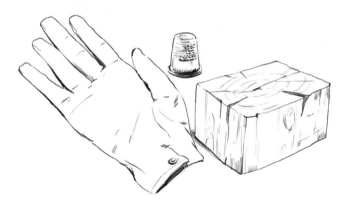

On it he had written: "And we'll wander through the wide world and chase the buffalo."

Charles might have been happy to play with his brothers and sisters forever. But when he was twelve, it was time for him to begin his formal education. Charles was going away to school.

CHAPTER 2
School Days

In 1844, Charles was sent to the Richmond School. He lived with the headmaster, who had six children of his own. In his first week at school Charles wrote to his sisters that the most popular games at the school were "foot-ball, wrestling, leap frog and fighting." He was only ten miles from Croft, but it must have felt much, much farther from home.

Sometimes bigger boys bullied the smaller ones. When Charles saw that happening he always tried to defend the smaller boy.

Although he didn't have much experience fighting, he became known as a defender of the weak. Later it was said that he "knew well how to use his fists in defense of a righteous cause."

Charles lived at Richmond for sixteen months. He won several prizes for good schoolwork. On his fourteenth birthday he left for Rugby, a boarding school for boys in central England. At that time Rugby was thought by many to be the best school in England.

Rugby School

The town of Rugby, where the school was located, was a much bigger city than Charles had ever lived in before.

What was life at Rugby like? Older boys were allowed to boss younger students around.

A new boy would be assigned to an older student and work for him—almost like a servant.

Rugby

When many people hear the word *rugby*, they don't think of the town or the school, but the game. Rugby was first played at the Rugby School in the nineteenth century. It may have been first invented in 1823 when a student disregarded the rules of soccer ("football" outside the United States), picked up the ball, and ran with it. Rugby looks a lot like American football with running, passing, and tackling—but until recently, no helmets or padding were worn. It is played with an oval ball.

There were strange traditions that new boys had to endure. For instance, a new boy would be forced to sing a song for older students. If they didn't like the boy's song, the boy had to drink something horrible, like a cup of toothpaste mixed with salt, mustard, and water. And the boys often played tricks on one another. A student might come back to his room and find everything upside down, with even his desk tied to the ceiling!

Charles spent three years at Rugby. And, just as at the Richmond School, he did well in his studies. His math teacher said of Charles, "I have not had a more promising boy at his age since I came to Rugby." Although he never complained about school, he wasn't very happy there. Years later he said, "I cannot say that I look back upon my life at a Public School with any sensations of pleasure, or that any earthly considerations would induce me to go through my three years again."

In 1849, Charles left Rugby for good. He was seventeen years old, and he hoped to attend the University of Oxford.

CHAPTER 3
Life in Oxford

Charles visited Oxford University in May 1850. But at that time there were no rooms available in the dormitory for him. So he returned home and planned to start school in January of the following year. Three days before his nineteenth birthday on January 24, 1851, he arrived at Oxford to begin his studies.

Oxford University was made up of thirty-eight unique colleges. Charles went to the one called Christ Church, where his father had gone.

Only two days after arriving at his new school, Charles got terrible news from home. His mother had died suddenly. Doctors called it an inflammation of the brain, which meant they weren't really sure what had happened. Charles's Aunt Lucy moved in with the family to help take care of the younger children. Charles returned to Oxford.

As a student at Christ Church, Charles wore a black robe over his clothes and a cap like the cap and gown students wear at graduation.

Christh Church College at Oxford University

No one knows the exact date when Oxford University was first founded. But there are records of teaching there as early as 1096. It's the oldest university in the English-speaking world. The college of Christ Church was founded in 1546 by King Henry VIII. It has produced thirteen British prime ministers among its graduates, more than any other college. The architecture and grounds of Christ Church College have been used as movie sets many times. The dining hall there was the inspiration for Hogwarts' Great Hall in the Harry Potter movies.

At night his rooms were lit by candles. As always, he worked hard at his math studies. He ended the year by earning a "first"—the highest marks a student could get.

The summer after his first year Charles went to visit his Uncle Skeffington in London. Charles and his uncle both loved gadgets, like microscopes and telescopes, and all sorts of inventions. Skeffington introduced Charles to his latest hobby: photography.

In 1839, a new process for developing pictures had been invented. Now people could take their own photographs. Charles was immediately interested in this new invention. It was the most cutting-edge technology in 1851.

Because of his good grades, Charles was awarded a studentship in December of 1851. This was a special honor at Christ Church. It meant that Charles would get a small salary. He would be able to live at Oxford as long as he wanted.

But he would also have new responsibilities. Charles was expected to take Holy Orders. That meant he would become a priest, like his father. Charles was very religious, so it seemed natural that he would follow in his father's footsteps. Usually, people gave up their studentship, their salary, and their free rooms only when they got married and started a family.

Charles had always liked writing funny

articles. The Dodgsons even created their own family newspaper. And Charles contributed poems, puzzles, stories, and drawings. When he was twenty-one, he began writing articles for real newspapers. But they were published without his name, so no one at that time knew he was the author.

Charles's stories were so popular that the editor of the *Comic Times*, a magazine that published funny stories and pictures, asked if he would begin signing his name to them.

Charles didn't want to use his real name because he wanted to keep his humorous stories separate from his more serious work—the math he worked on at Christ Church College. So the editor asked him to invent a pen name, a name that he would use just for his writing. Charles started out by scrambling versions of his own name and came up with Edgar Cuthwellis and Edgar U.C. Westhill. Then he tried out other names he liked the sound of. He sent his editor a list of ideas. In the end the editor chose Lewis Carroll. From then on whenever Charles wrote something that wasn't about math he signed it Lewis Carroll.

Charles graduated from Christ Church in 1854, with honors for his good grades. Many pupils left Oxford after

Why Lewis Carroll?

How do you get the name Lewis Carroll from Charles Lutwidge Dodgson? At Oxford, Charles studied Latin, and he seems to have put it to good use in choosing his pen name. Charles's middle name was Ludovicus in Latin. The English form of Ludovicus is Lewis. The name "Charles" comes from the same Latin name as Carroll: Carolus. So Charles Lutwidge in Latin is Carolus Ludovicus. Translate that name into English and you get Carroll Lewis—which Charles reversed to *Lewis Carroll.*

they got their degree. But Charles planned to stay. He would become one of the many scholars who lived and studied and taught at Oxford all their lives. He still received a salary for his studentship. Now Charles was twenty-two, and he was ready to begin his teaching career.

CHAPTER 4
Taking Pictures

A year after Charles graduated, Christ Church College got a new dean named Henry George Liddell. The dean was the person in charge of running the school. He was also the head of Christ Church cathedral, the church attached to the college, and Charles's new boss.

Henry George Liddell

Henry George Liddell (1811–1898)

Henry George Liddell was the headmaster, or principal, of Westminster School for boys before becoming dean of Christ Church, Oxford, in 1855. That same year he published a book called *History of Ancient Rome*. With his co-author, Robert Scott, he had earlier published a Greek-English dictionary that is still used today.

Henry Liddell was married to Lorina Reeve. Together, they had ten children: Harry, Lorina, Arthur, Alice, Edith, Rhoda, Albert, Violet, Frederick, and Lionel.

In February 1856, Charles went down to the river that ran through Oxford, to watch some boat races. This part of the Thames River was known as the Isis. At the races he met Mrs. Liddell, the new dean's wife. She was with her sister and two of her children, Harry and Lorina.

Charles was glad to meet Mrs. Liddell, but
he got along better with the children, especially
Harry. Eight-year-old Harry sometimes struggled
with math, so Charles offered to tutor him.
Through Harry, Charles eventually met all of the
Liddell children.

The Boat Race

Every year in early spring the Oxford University
Boat Club and the Cambridge University Boat Club
race along a course that is a little over four miles
on the Thames River from Putney to Mortlake. The
first race was held in 1829 and it's been held almost
every year since 1856. Each boat—called an "eight"—

has a team of eight rowers who work the long oars on either side. Each team must work well together in order to move the boat quickly through the water.

More than 250,000 people gather on the shore annually to watch the race, which is also known as the Oxford and Cambridge University Boat Race.

Around this same time, Charles was becoming more and more interested in photography. In March he went to London and bought a new camera. It was very expensive—15 pounds (about $1,700 today.) For some people in the 1850s, that might have been a whole year's salary! But Charles thought it was worth it. He was completely enchanted with this new technology.

Charles wanted to take pictures of people he knew, including the Liddell children. And no one was a better model than Alice Liddell. She was four years old. She had short dark hair. And she thought dressing up in costumes and having her picture taken was a lot of fun.

Photography at that time was very different than it is today. It didn't happen with the click of a button. In those days, people had to stay perfectly still for almost a minute! If they moved even slightly, their image in the photograph would be blurry.

While they patiently waited in front of the camera, Charles told the children funny stories to keep their attention. A friend once asked him how he managed to keep a child from fidgeting.

He said, "I wedge her into the corner of a room, if standing, or into the angle of a sofa, if lying down." In other words, he tried to prop them up so they could sit or stand still long enough.

Charles photographed Alice and her sisters in all sorts of costumes—Chinese robes, fairy queen dresses, and even tattered beggars' clothes.

But there was something special about the pictures of Alice. The way she looked directly at the camera, with a spark in her eyes, made people wonder what she was thinking.

Charles returned to the Liddell home again and again to photograph the children. He took pictures of other people, too. Many important people came to Oxford. And Charles often showed them his albums full of photographs. Most people were fascinated by them. Many had never been photographed themselves and thought it sounded exciting.

Charles often asked visitors to sit and have their portraits taken by him. He photographed the Crown Prince of Denmark, the writer John Ruskin, and the artist Dante Gabriel Rossetti. While on vacation in Scotland, Charles met the famous poet Alfred, Lord Tennyson. Charles even photographed Tennyson with his niece dressed as Little Red Riding Hood.

Alfred, Lord Tennyson (1809–1892)

Alfred, Lord Tennyson and his two older brothers started writing poetry when they were teenagers. As an adult Alfred's poetry was very popular, and in 1850 he became poet laureate of England. The poet laureate was specially appointed by the queen to write poetry for important occasions. Some of his most famous poems include "The Lady of Shalott," "Ulysses," and "The Charge of the Light Brigade."

Because Charles had grown up entertaining his younger brothers and sisters, being with the Liddell children made him feel like he was at home with his own family. And there were many other children in and around Oxford whom Charles considered friends.

He tutored some and photographed others, but he saw them all as extensions of his own family. He loved their innocent way of looking at the world. And Charles did seem to have a special talent for entertaining children.

Over the Christmas holidays in 1856, he visited his family and took part in a show for his father's students. Charles loved going to the theater to see plays. Now he had his own chance to perform. He sang songs. He used different voices to play different characters. And he put on a Magic Lantern show. This was a type of slide projector that used an oil or gas-burning lamp to show images on the wall. Charles was able to make the pictures move simply by moving the projector. This was Charles's version of "special effects," and the children loved it. Charles loved it, too. He had as much fun as they did—as much fun as when he was a boy himself.

CHAPTER 5
A Day on the River

In addition to teaching at Oxford, Charles also taught math to younger children in the town for extra money. He liked tutoring children better than teaching college students. The Oxford students often didn't care about math. Some of them thought his lectures were boring. But with younger students Charles could see their excitement when they started to understand numbers.

Perhaps he still remembered that day when he had asked his father to explain math equations and was told he was too young to understand it. Charles really wanted to explain complicated math ideas in a way that ordinary people could understand. In 1860, Charles published a book about math. Then he published a series of study guides that were meant to help students pass their exams.

But life at Oxford wasn't all numbers and tests. In December 1860, the Liddells invited a special guest to visit them at Christ Church: Queen Victoria herself! Her son Albert, the Prince of Wales, was then a student at Christ Church College.

The Liddells hosted a party for the queen, and
Charles was invited to show his photographs to
the prince.

Queen Victoria (1819–1901)

Princess Alexandrina Victoria became queen when she was just eighteen years old. As Queen Victoria, she ruled the United Kingdom of Great Britain and Ireland from June 1837 until her death in 1901. Her reign—known as the Victorian Era— was a time of peace and prosperity. It was also a time of many great advances in science, industry, engineering, and medicine.

When Charles accepted his studentship at Christ Church, he had agreed to first become a deacon. This is a lower job than a parson or priest in the church. And so Charles became a deacon in December 1861. He would now be called Reverend Dodgson.

Most deacons went on to become priests within a year. Everyone expected Charles to do that, too, especially his friend Dean Liddell. But in October 1862, Charles confessed to Dean Liddell that he just didn't think he could become a priest.

Charles saw himself as an ordinary man. Although he loved the church very much, he didn't think he was special enough to be a role model for others. Dean Liddell decided to bend the rules. He allowed Charles to keep his studentship and remain a deacon.

The following summer in 1862, Charles took Alice, Edith, and Lorina boating on the river. His friend the Reverend Robinson Duckworth, who was also a teacher, came with them.

As they rowed, Charles told a story about Alice chasing a white rabbit down a rabbit hole into a strange and silly-sounding new world.

Robinson enjoyed the story as much as the children. He asked Charles where he had

Reverend Robinson Duckworth

heard it and was surprised when Charles told him he was making it up as they went along. When they got home that day Alice asked Charles to write down the story that he had told them. Charles promised that he would. That promise would change his life forever.

CHAPTER 6
Alice in Wonderland

Charles began writing *Alice's Adventures Under Ground* right away. He thought that was a good title because the girl in the story falls down a deep rabbit hole at the very beginning. He drew his own pictures to go with it.

Charles finished his book and gave it to Alice Liddell for Christmas in 1864. She was twelve.

Alexander Macmillan

Now that Charles had written the story down, he wondered if maybe other children would like to read it, too. Through a friend he met Alexander Macmillan, a publisher. Luckily, Macmillan agreed to publish Charles's book. But Charles would have to pay for the printing himself.

The book Charles gave to Macmillan was not exactly the same story as the one he wrote for Alice. Charles made a lot of changes, created new characters, and added new adventures.

The story that Charles wrote for Alice eventually became *Alice's Adventures in Wonderland*. In the book, seven-year-old Alice chases a white rabbit down a hole. She finds herself in a strange place she's never seen before. When Alice tries to make her way home, the journey and the story only get more complicated. She drinks from a bottle that makes her shrink to the size of a mouse. She finds a baby that turns into a pig before her eyes. And she attends a never-ending tea party. Along the way, Alice meets many unusual animals and people.

Alice finally makes her way to the ruler of Wonderland, the Queen of Hearts. When the queen orders Alice's head to be chopped off, she's not afraid. The queen and all her soldiers are only characters from a deck of playing cards.

When Charles was satisfied with the story, he contacted John Tenniel to illustrate the book.

Alice, the Queen of Hearts, and one of her soldiers

When John Tenniel saw the first copies of Charles's book, now called *Alice's Adventures in Wonderland*, he didn't like the way his illustrations had been printed. So Charles threw away all two thousand copies and had them printed again. Charles didn't really expect to earn any money from the book, but he cared deeply about the story and wanted the book to look as good as possible.

Characters in Wonderland

- **The White Rabbit— The frantic white rabbit is always late for something. He is constantly checking his pocket watch. The White Rabbit leads Alice to Wonderland.**

- **The Cheshire Cat—This is a cat who is always smiling. He explains how Wonderland works to Alice. And sometimes he disappears, leaving only his grin behind.**

- **The March Hare—This is a different sort of rabbit who is silly and loud. The March Hare is a guest at the Hatter's tea party. He likes to tease Alice.**

- **The Queen of Hearts**—The ruler of Wonderland is unpleasant. Her favorite order is "Off with their heads!" She does not like people who make her angry.

- **The Hatter**—A hatter is a person who makes hats. This hatter is sometimes very rude and *always* thinks it's time for tea.

John Tenniel (1820–1914)

Growing up in London, John Tenniel had been a quiet boy. He studied at the Royal Academy of Arts, but he left school and instead taught himself by copying the sketches and paintings of well-known artists. He became famous drawing cartoons for *Punch*, a British humor magazine, and was one of the most popular illustrators of his time. Tenniel drew political cartoons that often made fun of politicians and the government. Today he's best known for the illustrations he did for Lewis Carroll's books *Alice's Adventures in Wonderland* and *Through the Looking-Glass.*

ALICE'S

ADVENTURES IN WONDERLAND

BY

LEWIS CARROLL

WITH FORTY TWO ILLUSTRATIONS

BY

JOHN TENNIEL

MACMILLAN AND CO.
1865

(The right of translation is reserved.)

Finally on November 9, 1865, the new editions
were ready. Charles sent a copy to Queen Victoria's
youngest daughter, Beatrice, who was eight years
old. He never guessed that soon every child in
England would want a copy of *Alice's Adventures
in Wonderland*.

CHAPTER 7
Alice Everywhere

On July 4, 1866, Alice Liddell received her own copy of *Alice's Adventures in Wonderland.* Charles had sent her the Macmillan book on the anniversary of the day he first told it to her. By then it had gotten a lot of reviews in newspapers and magazines—all of them very good.

Alice was full of nonsense words and crazy characters. The character named Alice was a smart girl who tried to figure things out herself instead of being told what to do by an adult. She was a child in a world full of silly characters based on some of the grown-ups that Charles actually knew. It was as if Charles was letting children know that he understood how strange adults could seem. This was a very different kind of children's book.

People had never heard a story like *Alice* before. Most children's books at the time were carefully written to teach children lessons. In fact, when Charles himself was a small boy, the books he read were nothing like *Alice*. They were full of rules to follow and warnings about what might happen if you didn't. Books about "children who had got burnt, and eaten up by wild beasts . . . all because they *would* not remember the simple rules . . ." *Alice's Adventures in Wonderland* was fun. And that was something entirely new.

Sales were steady at first. And then they really took off. People who read it told their friends what a great story it was and then they wanted to read it, too. Children asked their parents to buy it. The book was translated into other languages to sell in foreign countries. A publisher in the United States put out its own version of the book that very same year without Charles's permission. He was not happy about it.

Charles was starting to become famous as an author. But sometimes it bothered him. He wanted to keep "Lewis Carroll," the author, separate from Charles Dodgson, the teacher and math book author. If someone called him Lewis Carroll he didn't answer. And he didn't accept letters addressed to Lewis Carroll at his Oxford address.

Charles was a familiar figure to all the children in Oxford. One little girl remembered a day when she was playing and another girl said, "Here comes Mr. Dodgson!" She looked down the road to see a tall man dressed in somber black clothes walking stiffly toward them. The children decided to play a joke. They linked hands to form a barrier so he couldn't get by. As he got close to them the dignified professor suddenly pulled out his umbrella and ran at them like a jousting knight.

The children scattered, then came back to grab onto him and walk with him, giggling and chattering like old friends.

Children were his favorite audience. He still made up stories to entertain his many young friends in Oxford. He even wrote letters back and forth with many of them, sometimes for years after they grew up.

Of course all his child friends loved *Alice's Adventures in Wonderland*. Charles started to think about writing another adventure for Alice. But first, he was going on an adventure of his own. For the first time in his life Charles was traveling outside of England. He decided to visit Russia.

In the 1860s, many English people traveled throughout Europe. But very few went so far as Russia. This was a very unusual choice for Charles, who thought this faraway country seemed full of mystery and romance. Charles was probably interested in Russia because he'd read about it in books. He decided to take the trip with his friend Henry Liddon, who was also a teacher at Christ Church.

Charles prepared very carefully for his trip. He carried a wallet that was divided into sections for the exact amount of money he would spend each day. He noted down how many paintings were in a gallery he went to in Germany (1,243),

and the exact time it took the train to get from Germany to St. Petersburg in Russia (28½ hours).

Charles had always loved numbers, and he couldn't resist keeping track of them.

Charles also wrote down foreign words that he liked the sound of. He tasted Russian food and drinks. He went to plays even though he couldn't understand the words. He carried a small telescope and sometimes ran up into bell towers to get a bird's-eye view of the streets below.

He kept a diary where he sketched the new people and landscapes he saw.

His diary was also filled with funny stories. One was about the time Liddon had asked a hotel maid to hold his coat. When it came time to get the coat back, the maid couldn't understand what Liddon wanted. She didn't speak English, and they didn't speak Russian. Charles acted out putting on a coat to help her understand. The maid would nod as if she did. But she brought him everything but the coat—a broom, a pillow, a cup of tea. Finally, Charles drew a picture for her, and Liddon got his coat back.

Charles described his travels in Russia as if he had stumbled into his own Wonderland filled with fantastic characters, churches with blue domes covered in gold stars, and cities that were so huge, they seemed as if they were built for giants.

Charles returned to Oxford in October 1867. About eight months later he received what he called the "greatest blow" of his life when his father died. Not only had he lost a father he loved and looked up to, but he quite suddenly became the head of the family. Charles had six sisters who were unmarried.

That meant he had to take care of them. Since
their home belonged to the church in Croft, the
family had to move.

Once he settled them into a new home not too far from Oxford, Charles himself moved into a bigger apartment at Oxford. By this time *Alice's*

Adventures in Wonderland was selling around six thousand copies a year just in England. Thanks to the money he earned from the book, Charles could afford to teach fewer classes. He had more time for photography and inventing little gadgets and games of his own. Some of his favorites included a portable chess game for travelers and a device to make it easier to read sideways in bed. Charles was always thinking up something new.

CHAPTER 9
Through the Looking-Glass

Charles was busy writing his new book about Alice. In this story, instead of falling down a rabbit hole, Alice found a strange, fantastic world on the other side of her mirror.

While he was writing, more translations of *Alice's Adventures in Wonderland* appeared in German, French, and Italian. Charles hoped everyone would like the new book, *Through the Looking-Glass and What Alice Found There*, just as much. John Tenniel got to work on new illustrations.

In June of 1870, Charles received a surprising visit. Mrs. Liddell brought her daughters Lorina and Alice to see him.

Alice was now eighteen years old. Charles had not seen her for seven years! He photographed her for the last time sitting in a chair. Alice wore a long dress. Her hair was piled on top of her head with a bow. She was barely recognizable as the short-haired little girl with bare feet in the garden whom Charles remembered.

But Charles still had many friends he had made when they were children and stayed friends with as adults. And Charles always worried about children who didn't have families to take care of them. He became involved with charities that worked with young people, caring for orphans and other children in need. He also joined a campaign to create a national acting school that finally opened in 1904 and is now known as the Royal Academy of Dramatic Art (RADA). Some of the most famous British actors have graduated from RADA.

Charles finished *Through the Looking-Glass and*  *What Alice Found There* in January 1871. Macmillan already had 7,500 orders for the book, and it hadn't even been published! They planned to print nine thousand copies to start.

RADA

The Royal Academy of Dramatic Art is one of the oldest acting schools in Great Britain and one of the most respected acting schools in the world. Students have to audition to get in, and the program only accepts around twenty-five people a year.

The school teaches acting as well as directing, stage design, and other jobs in the theater. Many famous actors went to RADA, including Alan Rickman, who played Severus Snape; Ralph Fiennes, who played Lord Voldemort; and Kenneth Branagh, who played Gilderoy Lockhart, from the Harry Potter films.

Charles loved Tenniel's new illustrations, but he did have one request. On the inside cover of the book the publisher had put a picture of the Jabberwock, an imaginary monster from a poem in the story. Charles thought that picture was too scary to go on the first page, so it was replaced with a picture of the character of the white knight.

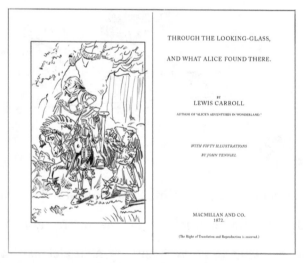

Through the Looking-Glass introduced readers to even more fantastic characters. There were the twins Tweedledum and Tweedledee,

the White Queen, and the White Knight. The Hatter, the March Hare, and Alice's cat Dinah from *Wonderland* also make appearances. And *Through the Looking-Glass* contained another now-famous poem, "The Walrus and the Carpenter," about two friends who walk along the beach while the sun shines in the middle of the night.

Seven weeks after *Through the Looking-Glass* came out, Macmillan reported to Charles that the book had sold fifteen thousand copies and he had orders for five hundred more. It was another big hit.

"Jabberwocky"

'Twas brillig, and the slithy toves
Did gyre and gimble in the wabe:
All mimsy were the borogoves,
And the mome raths outgrabe.

So begins one of Lewis Carroll's most famous poems. It's the story of a young hero who goes into the woods with his sword to slay the terrible Jabberwock with its jaws that bite and claws that catch.

In *Through the Looking-Glass*, Alice can only read the poem when she holds it up to a mirror. Unfortunately the poem is just as confusing to Alice  either way. "Jabberwocky" is considered to be one of the greatest nonsense poems of all time. And it has been a favorite of young readers for more than a hundred years.

Although he was now a successful author, Charles's life hadn't changed much. He took an eighteen-mile walk every day for exercise. He visited with his friends, and stayed close to his family. In the summer of 1874, Charles went to visit Charlie Wilcox. Charlie was Charles's cousin and also his godson. Charlie was very sick. Sometimes he couldn't sleep, and Charles stayed up with him. One day after spending all night awake with Charlie, Charles went outside for some fresh air. As he was walking, a line of poetry popped into his head: "For the Snark *was* a Boojum, you see."

Charlie died only a few months later. Charles continued to work on the poem. He called it *The Hunting of the Snark*. To some it's a nonsense poem about a group of ten silly hunters chasing an imaginary beast. But others have puzzled over the true meaning of the poem. Charles himself once noted that it was a story about the search for happiness, and also a comment that maybe happiness can never truly be caught.

The Hunting of the Snark was published with illustrations by Henry Holiday in the spring of 1876.

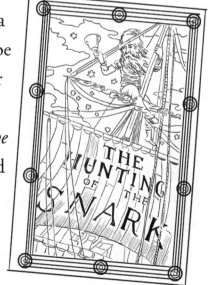

Since its publication, *The Hunting of the Snark* has inspired musicals, operas, plays, music, short stories, anime, science fiction, and video games. Not bad for a lot of "nonsense."

Portmanteau Words

A portmanteau combines more than one word to make up a new word. Sometimes sounds—as well as words—are combined. In *Through the Looking-Glass*, the character Humpty Dumpty explains the practice of combining words by telling Alice: "You see it's like a portmanteau—there are two meanings packed up into one word."

Here are a few examples of Lewis Carroll's portmanteau words:

- chuckle + snort = *chortle*, a noisy laugh
- gallop + triumph = *galumph*, to march proudly and clumsily
- fuming + furious = *frumious*, very angry
- fair + joyous = *frabjous*, great, wonderful

The word *portmanteau* itself is a portmanteau! It is made of the French word for *carry* + the French word for *coat* = a suitcase that carries clothing. Or, in Lewis Carroll's world, "two meanings packed up into one word."

CHAPTER 10
Alice Forever

By 1880, photography had become a much more popular hobby. There were new ways of developing photographs that were much simpler than the old process Charles used. It was not uncommon for a person to have their picture taken at a professional studio. As others grew more interested in photography, it seemed that Charles lost his interest completely. He took his last picture in July 1880. That same month he decided to resign as a math lecturer. He would no longer be teaching classes at Oxford but he would continue to live there.

Charles still had a busy life. He lived in a building with other scholars and they shared a sitting room called the Common Room. They took turns holding the job of curator of the Common Room. The curator was in charge of things like daily menus, ordering the wine, and making sure that anything that needed repairs got fixed.

In 1882, Charles became the curator of the Common Room at Christ Church. He took the job very seriously and felt good about making their home more pleasant for everyone. This job was perfect for Charles because he always liked everything neat and tidy. For instance, as soon as he got the job he decided to make improvements with what he called "Airs, Glares, and Chairs." That is—better windows, better lighting, and new armchairs.

While Charles's life was changing at Oxford, Alice Liddell's life was changing, too. She was now married and lived far away from Oxford. One day Charles unexpectedly ran into Alice when she was visiting her family in Oxford. She agreed to lend Charles the original, handwritten copy of *Alice's Adventures Under Ground*. Charles wanted to publish that version, too. That way people could see the original story that inspired the book they loved so much.

When a playwright named Henry Savile Clarke asked Charles if he could turn his first book into an operetta with songs, Charles happily

agreed. He had always loved the theater and was thrilled to have one of his stories become a musical play. It was exciting for him to see his own work onstage. *Alice in Wonderland: A Musical Dream Play* premiered at the Prince of Wales Theater in December 1886. One of the girls who played Alice was Isa Bowman, and she and Charles naturally became great friends.

By the time Charles was in his fifties, he spent much more time with adults than with children. He had many friends with whom he went to plays and out to dinner. And he—as always—remained interested in all the latest inventions. In May 1888, he became one of the first people in Oxford to own a typewriter. Just a few years later, he traveled to an exhibition in London where he first saw a phonograph, a device for playing recorded music. Charles was amazed!

As the *Alice* books got more and more popular, other writers were eager to link themselves to Wonderland. There were suddenly a lot of new children's books written about characters finding their own secret worlds.

The *Alice* books also inspired a lot of related products. In 1888, Charles designed a Wonderland Stamp Case. It was a lot like the wallets he took with him when traveling. There were different pockets, each to hold a different stamp. What made it special were the illustrations from *Alice in Wonderland*. On the outside was a picture of Alice holding the baby from

Wonderland, and a picture of the Cheshire Cat. A cardboard panel inside the case showed the

baby transformed into a pig and the cat all but disappeared.

There were Alice-themed toys, including jigsaw puzzles, slides for magic lanterns, and card games. And for adults, a carved-ivory umbrella handle shaped like Tweedledee and Tweedledum.

When he was sixty, Charles began writing a series of books about math logic that could be understood by people who were not math students. The first volume was published in 1896. It was called *Symbolic Logic Part I*.

At sixty-five, Charles still lived much as he always had, taking a long walk every day, visiting with friends, going to the theater, and spending time talking with children.

In 1897, Charles went to see his family for Christmas. He caught a bad cold that only got worse. Eventually, it turned into pneumonia. On January 14, 1898, Charles died in his family's home, surrounded by the brothers and sisters whom he'd made so happy as children. When the doctor came to see him one last time he said to the family, "How wonderfully young your brother looks!" In many ways, Charles *was* still young to them. His brothers and sisters had never stopped thinking of him as the curious, bright young boy he had once been.

By the time Charles died, children all over the world knew and had been delighted by his stories. Those who had been lucky enough to know him would never forget him. He was like no other adult. Some part of him would always belong to children.

Alice's Adventures in Wonderland and *Through the Looking-Glass and What Alice Found There* are still sold all over the world today. *Alice's Adventures in Wonderland* has been translated into 174 languages, including Arabic and Zulu. This incredibly popular book has also been adapted into many film and TV versions.

No matter how many new versions of *Alice in Wonderland* are made, the book itself is still just as popular. In 2015, Macmillan publishers celebrated its 150th anniversary by printing a special edition of the book. They held a contest for artists to create a new illustration for the cover. Celebrations were held all over the world. But maybe the most unique one was in Oxford, where people took a special boat ride on the Isis on July 4 to commemorate that day a hundred  and fifty years earlier when the story of Alice was born.

Disney's *Alice*

When many people think of Alice, they picture Walt Disney's animated film version. But at the time of its release in 1951, Walt Disney Studio's *Alice in Wonderland* was not a big success. Fans of Lewis Carroll thought that Disney had "Americanized" a great work of English literature.

But the movie has gone on to become one of Disney's great animated classics.

Disney's *Alice* is so popular that all of the company's theme parks feature the teacup ride which was inspired by the movie.

Timeline of Lewis Carroll's Life

1832	Charles Lutwidge Dodgson (later known as Lewis Carroll) is born in Daresbury, England
1843	Dodgson family moves to Croft, England
1844	Goes to Richmond School
1846	Goes to Rugby School
1851	Enters Christ Church, Oxford University
1856	Meets Alice Liddell
1862	Begins the story of Alice in Wonderland
1865	*Alice's Adventures in Wonderland* is published
1867	Travels to Russia
1871	*Through the Looking-Glass and What Alice Found There* is published
1876	*The Hunting of the Snark* is published
1886	*Alice in Wonderland: A Musical Dream Play* premieres in London
1888	Buys his first typewriter
1898	Dies in Guildford, England

Timeline of the World

1832	First horse-drawn streetcar in New York City
1835	Concepción, Chile, is destroyed by an earthquake
1839	Louis Daguerre takes the first photograph of the moon
1843	First wagon train leaves from Missouri for Oregon
1852	First edition of *Roget's Thesaurus* is published
1853	Harriet Tubman begins transporting slaves to freedom as part of the Underground Railroad
1855	The Bunsen burner is invented
1857	The Sheffield Football Club, the first soccer club, is founded in England
1883	Buffalo Bill puts on the first Wild West Show in Omaha, Nebraska
1885	Washington Monument opens in Washington, DC
1889	Eiffel Tower opens
1892	The town of St. John's, Newfoundland, destroyed by fire
1894	The Kellogg brothers create cornflakes in Battle Creek, Michigan

Bibliography

* Books for young readers

* Bassett, Lisa. *Very Truly Yours, Charles L. Dodgson, Alias Lewis Carroll.* New York: Lothrop, Lee & Shepard Books, 1987.

Bethune, Brian. "Curiouser and Curiouser: 150 Years of Alice in Wonderland." *Mclean's*, May 29, 2015. http://www.macleans.ca/culture/books/curiouser-and-curiouser-150-years-of-alice-in-wonderland.

Cohen, Morton N. *Lewis Carroll: A Biography.* New York: Vintage Books, 1995.

Douglas-Fairhurst, Robert. *The Story of Alice: Lewis Carroll and the Secret History of Wonderland.* Cambridge: Belknap Press, 2015.

Lane, Anthony. "Go Ask Alice: What Really Went on in Wonderland." *New Yorker*, June 8 & 15, 2015.

* Stoffel, Stephanie Lovett. *Lewis Carroll in Wonderland: The Life and Times of Alice and Her Creator.* New York: Harry N. Abrams, 1997.

Woolf, Jenny. *The Mystery of Lewis Carroll: Discovering the Whimsical, Thoughtful, and Sometimes Lonely Man Who Created Alice in Wonderland.* New York: St. Martin's, 2010.